Stepping
Into Wholeness

A Guided Journal

Dr. Sharon Sanders-Funnye

Dedication

This journal is dedicated to the many mothers, grandmothers, and othermothers who pour so much of themselves, their wisdom, and their stories into us throughout our lives. It is because of them that we are able to live WHOLE lives today. Their past experiences teach us today and always. Their legacy continues.

A Gift from ME to YOU

As you read the brief quips and anecdotes, you will smile, laugh, think deeply, be encouraged, understand, remember, and feel the need to act. Reading is only half of the equation. The other half involves the recording of your thoughts, actions, and the change that you will create for the world to experience.

Most importantly,

Your Journey to WHOLENESS Has Begun!

Say It Is and It is So!

Let the words that pass from your heart through your mouth speak life, blessing, and confidence.

What do YOU say about YOU, Your Life, and Your Future this day?

_____

_____

_____

_____

_____

_____

_____

_____

_____

_____

_____

_____

Freedom is activated by your thoughts, is released
throughout your body, and radiates from your spirit.

_____

_____

_____

_____

_____

_____

_____

_____

_____

_____

_____

_____

_____

_____

Your Journey to Wholeness Has Begun

Freedom is activated by your thoughts, is released
throughout your body, and radiates from your spirit.

_____

_____

_____

_____

_____

_____

_____

_____

_____

_____

_____

_____

_____

_____

_____

_____

_____

_____

_____

_____

Your Journey to Wholeness Has Begun

Be at Your Best

Who is your biggest fan? YOU. This doesn't mean you have to go around bragging, but if you won't put yourself first, who will? Each week, think about three things that you love about yourself and share them in this journal.

Freedom is activated by your thoughts, is released throughout your body, and radiates from your spirit.

_____

_____

_____

_____

_____

_____

_____

_____

_____

_____

Your Journey to Wholeness Has Begun

Freedom is activated by your thoughts, is released throughout your body, and radiates from your spirit.

_____

_____

_____

_____

_____

_____

_____

_____

_____

_____

_____

_____

_____

_____

_____

_____

Your Journey to Wholeness Has Begun

Freedom is activated by your thoughts, is released
throughout your body, and radiates from your spirit.

_____

_____

_____

_____

_____

_____

_____

_____

_____

_____

_____

_____

_____

_____

_____

Your Journey to Wholeness Has Begun

Treat Others the Way
You Want to be Treated

Are you honoring yourself today…your spirit, body, and mind? If you want to treat others well, that is good. Consider doing the same for yourself. Don't let a day go by without loving yourself.

On a scale of 1-10, rate your treatment of yourself. If your number is below an 8, you have work to do. Are you willing to do the work?

_____

_____

_____

_____

_____

_____

_____

_____

_____

_____

Freedom is activated by your thoughts, is released
throughout your body, and radiates from your spirit.

_____

_____

_____

_____

_____

_____

_____

_____

_____

_____

_____

_____

_____

_____

_____

Your Journey to Wholeness Has Begun

Freedom is activated by your thoughts, is released
throughout your body, and radiates from your spirit.

_____

_____

_____

_____

_____

_____

_____

_____

_____

_____

_____

_____

_____

_____

Your Journey to Wholeness Has Begun

A Little Kindness Goes a Long Way

A grain of sand or a morsel of salt, both may be
found in a beach. The beach is made up of grains
of sand and the ocean is made up of salt water.
The beauty of all of it is that it began with a little.
Be kind to yourself today and then spread your
kindness around. You will feel better and you
could be the bright spot in someone else's day.

Will you let your light shine?

_____

_____

_____

_____

_____

_____

_____

_____

_____

_____

Freedom is activated by your thoughts, is released
throughout your body, and radiates from your spirit.

_____

_____

_____

_____

_____

_____

_____

_____

_____

_____

_____

_____

_____

_____

_____

_____

Your Journey to Wholeness Has Begun

Freedom is activated by your thoughts, is released
throughout your body, and radiates from your spirit.

_____

_____

_____

_____

_____

_____

_____

_____

_____

_____

_____

_____

_____

_____

_____

Your Journey to Wholeness Has Begun

Your Word Is You

Have you ever contemplated that people may perceive your character by the words that come out of your mouth? If every word that came from you was automatically glowing on your head, everyone would know what you were thinking.

Would the words be empowering or would your words be defeating? What will you change, if anything?

_____

_____

_____

_____

_____

_____

_____

_____

_____

_____

_____

Freedom is activated by your thoughts, is released
throughout your body, and radiates from your spirit.

_____

_____

_____

_____

_____

_____

_____

_____

_____

_____

_____

_____

_____

_____

Your journey to Wholeness Has Begun

Freedom is activated by your thoughts, is released
throughout your body, and radiates from your spirit.

_____

_____

_____

_____

_____

_____

_____

_____

_____

_____

_____

_____

_____

_____

_____

_____

_____

Your Journey to Wholeness Has Begun

Your New Thing

We've all heard the cliché 'your new normal,' but what has it meant for you? Is there something you'd like to leave in your past to create a new normal? Share your 'new thing' here now.

Declare it in writing and go forward.

_____

_____

_____

_____

_____

_____

_____

_____

_____

_____

_____

_____

Freedom is activated by your thoughts, is released
throughout your body, and radiates from your spirit.

_____

_____

_____

_____

_____

_____

_____

_____

_____

_____

_____

_____

_____

_____

_____

_____

Your Journey to Wholeness Has Begun

Freedom is activated by your thoughts, is released
throughout your body, and radiates from your spirit.

Your Journey to Wholeness Has Begun

Get Up off of Your Thang

Feeling a little blue today, not like your usual
self? Then, this is the time to ramp up. Get up.
Speak positive words to yourself, OUT LOUD.
Walk it out!

Ultimately, what will you do?

_____

_____

_____

_____

_____

_____

_____

_____

_____

_____

_____

_____

_____

Freedom is activated by your thoughts, is released
throughout your body, and radiates from your spirit.

_____

_____

_____

_____

_____

_____

_____

_____

_____

_____

_____

_____

_____

_____

Your Journey to Wholeness Has Begun

Freedom is activated by your thoughts, is released
throughout your body, and radiates from your spirit.

_____

_____

_____

_____

_____

_____

_____

_____

_____

_____

_____

_____

_____

_____

_____

_____

Your Journey to Wholeness Has Begun

Get Out of Your Feelings

So, your emotions have taken you over, huh?
You're feeling a little at odds with yourself or a
situation you're dealing with. How will you
handle it? Here's a suggestion: breathe. Let it out,
and suck it up.

Will you allow your negative emotions to flow
far away from you? Try it now, and write about
how you feel so you can release.

_____

_____

_____

_____

_____

_____

_____

_____

_____

_____

Freedom is activated by your thoughts, is released
throughout your body, and radiates from your spirit.

_____

_____

_____

_____

_____

_____

_____

_____

_____

_____

_____

_____

_____

_____

_____

_____

Your Journey to Wholeness Has Begun

Freedom is activated by your thoughts, is released
throughout your body, and radiates from your spirit.

_____

_____

_____

_____

_____

_____

_____

_____

_____

_____

_____

_____

_____

_____

_____

Your Journey to Wholeness Has Begun

Reflection of Yourself

It's easy to blame others for what doesn't work out well. The question is: have you been accountable for your part in it? Look in the Mirror. Think about your Actions. You will see your true self, or think of who YOU really are.

Would YOU CHANGE anything?

_____

_____

_____

_____

_____

_____

_____

_____

_____

_____

_____

_____

Freedom is activated by your thoughts, is released throughout your body, and radiates from your spirit.

_____

_____

_____

_____

_____

_____

_____

_____

_____

_____

_____

_____

_____

_____

_____

_____

Your Journey to Wholeness Has Begun

Freedom is activated by your thoughts, is released throughout your body, and radiates from your spirit.

_____

_____

_____

_____

_____

_____

_____

_____

_____

_____

_____

_____

_____

_____

_____

_____

Your Journey to Wholeness Has Begun

Learn, Grow, Do, Learn...

Every day presents an opportunity for us to learn more, grow a little more, do a little more, and learn more all over again.

What did you learn last month? How did you grow last week? What did you do yesterday? What would you like to learn today?

_____

_____

_____

_____

_____

_____

_____

_____

_____

_____

_____

Freedom is activated by your thoughts, is released throughout your body, and radiates from your spirit.

_____

_____

_____

_____

_____

_____

_____

_____

_____

_____

_____

_____

_____

_____

_____

Your Journey to Wholeness Has Begun

Freedom is activated by your thoughts, is released throughout your body, and radiates from your spirit.

_____

_____

_____

_____

_____

_____

_____

_____

_____

_____

_____

_____

_____

_____

_____

Your Journey to Wholeness Has Begun

Grandma-ism
"If You Don't Listen to Me, You Will Listen to Somebody."

My grandmother used to say this all the time. Accountability can sometimes be difficult, especially when what you want to do is not the best thing for you to do. Ever seek wise counsel or a mentor, just to get another's opinion? Find someone you trust and ask their thoughts. Ultimately, you get to decide, but you owe it to yourself to make the BEST decision for YOU.

What will it be?

_____

_____

_____

_____

_____

_____

_____

_____

_____

_____

Freedom is activated by your thoughts, is released throughout your body, and radiates from your spirit.

_____

_____

_____

_____

_____

_____

_____

_____

_____

_____

_____

_____

_____

_____

_____

Your Journey to Wholeness Has Begun

Freedom is activated by your thoughts, is released
throughout your body, and radiates from your spirit.

_____

_____

_____

_____

_____

_____

_____

_____

_____

_____

_____

_____

_____

_____

Your Journey to Wholeness Has Begun

Master It First, Before Moving On

Everyone wants to move up in position or stature. One glance at social media and it becomes clear we all want more and we want it now. Before moving up and on, complete the process. Once you complete and master the process, it is a prime time to move forward.

What have you mastered and what's your next move?

_____

_____

_____

_____

_____

_____

_____

_____

_____

_____

_____

Freedom is activated by your thoughts, is released
throughout your body, and radiates from your spirit.

_____

_____

_____

_____

_____

_____

_____

_____

_____

_____

_____

_____

_____

_____

Your Journey to Wholeness Has Begun

Freedom is activated by your thoughts, is released
throughout your body, and radiates from your spirit.

_____

_____

_____

_____

_____

_____

_____

_____

_____

_____

_____

_____

_____

_____

_____

Your Journey to Wholeness Has Begun

Relax the Relationship

I was friends with someone for about 4 years. I liked that she always had new ideas, but her follow-through was always a little shaky. What I learned was that she wanted to have her cake and wanted to eat the whole thing, too. Meaning, there was no room to share. As I was reflecting early one morning, I heard, in my spirit, 'relax the relationship,' meaning I needed to take a break or let it go.

Is there a relationship you're in that needs to be relaxed?

_____

_____

_____

_____

_____

_____

_____

_____

_____

Freedom is activated by your thoughts, is released throughout your body, and radiates from your spirit.

_____

_____

_____

_____

_____

_____

_____

_____

_____

_____

_____

_____

_____

_____

_____

Your Journey to Wholeness Has Begun

Freedom is activated by your thoughts, is released throughout your body, and radiates from your spirit.

_____

_____

_____

_____

_____

_____

_____

_____

_____

_____

_____

_____

_____

_____

_____

Your Journey to Wholeness Has Begun

Don't Overthink It!

As a Type A Personality, I have a tendency to overthink things. I am probably seeking perfection, which doesn't exist. What I have learned is that in my effort to 'get it right,' I may lose some of the passion and enjoyment on the way to perfection. It's okay to live in the moment sometimes, as long as there's no harm to yourself or others. Let go and let it flow.

Is there something you need to be okay with or something you need to accept?

_____

_____

_____

_____

_____

_____

_____

_____

_____

_____

Freedom is activated by your thoughts, is released throughout your body, and radiates from your spirit.

_____

_____

_____

_____

_____

_____

_____

_____

_____

_____

_____

_____

_____

_____

_____

Your Journey to Wholeness Has Begun

Freedom is activated by your thoughts, is released
throughout your body, and radiates from your spirit.

_____

_____

_____

_____

_____

_____

_____

_____

_____

_____

_____

_____

_____

_____

_____

_____

Your Journey to Wholeness Has Begun

Plan with Purpose and Priority

Is there an idea that won't let go of you? You go to bed and wake up, thinking of it. Why do you think that is? Experience tells me that it's in your spirit and it will keep crying out to you until you acknowledge it. Pray about it, understand the purpose for it, and prioritize time to pursue it.

What is the idea or concept, and what will you do about it?

_____

_____

_____

_____

_____

_____

_____

_____

_____

_____

_____

Freedom is activated by your thoughts, is released
throughout your body, and radiates from your spirit.

_____

_____

_____

_____

_____

_____

_____

_____

_____

_____

_____

_____

_____

_____

_____

Your Journey to Wholeness Has Begun

Freedom is activated by your thoughts, is released
throughout your body, and radiates from your spirit.

_____

_____

_____

_____

_____

_____

_____

_____

_____

_____

_____

_____

_____

_____

Your Journey to Wholeness Has Begun

High Expectations

Expectations are a funny thing. Sometimes you expect more of others than they are capable of giving. At other times, it's YOU who may fall short of someone else's expectations, maybe at work, on a team, or in a group. Either way, EXPECTATIONS may push us to get it done! Expectations may be the catalyst for ACHIEVEMENT.

Think of ONE expectation you have for yourself and write it down. Now, begin to list the steps you will take to make it happen!

_____

_____

_____

_____

_____

_____

_____

_____

_____

Freedom is activated by your thoughts, is released
throughout your body, and radiates from your spirit.

_____

_____

_____

_____

_____

_____

_____

_____

_____

_____

_____

_____

_____

_____

_____

Your Journey to Wholeness Has Begun

Freedom is activated by your thoughts, is released
throughout your body, and radiates from your spirit.

_____

_____

_____

_____

_____

_____

_____

_____

_____

_____

_____

_____

_____

_____

_____

Your Journey to Wholeness Has Begun

Paralysis Destroys Productivity

Ever feel stuck in a situation or circumstance? Think of what's stopping you from making forward movement. What has stopped you from producing something good or something that you would be proud of? Is it fear or lack of resources? Where there is opportunity, there is an open door.

To be productive, you must enter or walk through the door, but are you willing to move? Take a risk!

_____

_____

_____

_____

_____

_____

_____

_____

_____

Freedom is activated by your thoughts, is released throughout your body, and radiates from your spirit.

_____

_____

_____

_____

_____

_____

_____

_____

_____

_____

_____

_____

_____

_____

_____

_____

Your Journey to Wholeness Has Begun

Freedom is activated by your thoughts, is released
throughout your body, and radiates from your spirit.

_____

_____

_____

_____

_____

_____

_____

_____

_____

_____

_____

_____

_____

_____

_____

Your Journey to Wholeness Has Begun

Value

For many years, I remained in a situation where I did not feel valued. Because my partner did not value me, I forgot to value myself. I continued to thrive, but one day, I realized I was simply doing whatever it took to please others, with little joy. I asked myself, 'Why is that?' I realized I had to see myself as a person of value and that it was okay to be happy about my contributions.

Are you feeling valued today? Write one element of value that you bring to the world. It could be that YOUR PRESENCE IS VALUABLE ENOUGH!

_____

_____

_____

_____

_____

_____

_____

_____

_____

Freedom is activated by your thoughts, is released
throughout your body, and radiates from your spirit.

_____

_____

_____

_____

_____

_____

_____

_____

_____

_____

_____

_____

_____

_____

Your Journey to Wholeness Has Begun

Freedom is activated by your thoughts, is released
throughout your body, and radiates from your spirit.

_____

_____

_____

_____

_____

_____

_____

_____

_____

_____

_____

_____

_____

_____

_____

_____

Your Journey to Wholeness Has Begun

Remember Who You Are

I married just after graduate school and moved to New York. I had taken a position with a Fortune 100 Company, had a new husband, and was on top of the world. Prior to leaving home, my mom shared the parting words, "Remember who you are." As she said them, I looked at her strangely and thought, *I know who I am. What is she talking about?* Fast forward, 23 years later and I thought of my mom's words. I realized she had wisdom that I did not have at that time. She had seen and experienced many things I had no knowledge of then. Today, I understand. It is easy to lose yourself in a relationship, in a career, or in a role you have in your family.

Ask yourself, do I remember who I am? Write your answer here.

_____

_____

_____

_____

_____

_____

Freedom is activated by your thoughts, is released
throughout your body, and radiates from your spirit.

_____

_____

_____

_____

_____

_____

_____

_____

_____

_____

_____

_____

_____

_____

_____

_____

Your Journey to Wholeness Has Begun

Freedom is activated by your thoughts, is released
throughout your body, and radiates from your spirit.

_____

_____

_____

_____

_____

_____

_____

_____

_____

_____

_____

_____

_____

_____

_____

Your Journey to Wholeness Has Begun

Grandma-ism

Charity Begins at Home and Spreads Abroad

All the grandchildren heard this while growing up. I think it was usually spoken when my grandmother observed the children acting like they had no home training. Perhaps it was a look, an attitude of disobedience, a slow response to a directive, or half-doing chores. Charity is the highest form of love, according to scripture, so when my grandmother said it, she must have meant we were not acting in a loving way of demonstrating a loving character, unselfishly. I think of my grandmother often and her quips and quotes, as well.

Are you showing CHARITY to others through your character and in your response to duties? Do a Charity Check-up and think of two areas in which you could improve. Yes, we all can improve at something.

_____

_____

_____

_____

Freedom is activated by your thoughts, is released
throughout your body, and radiates from your spirit.

_____

_____

_____

_____

_____

_____

_____

_____

_____

_____

_____

_____

_____

_____

_____

Your Journey to Wholeness Has Begun

Freedom is activated by your thoughts, is released
throughout your body, and radiates from your spirit.

_____

_____

_____

_____

_____

_____

_____

_____

_____

_____

_____

_____

_____

_____

_____

Your Journey to Wholeness Has Begun

Just Stop and Breathe

I woke up one morning and could barely catch my breath. This had never happened to me, so I questioned why. I questioned if I was having a panic attack or not. Yes, I was under stress at work with projects and deadlines, but what was this about? Then wisdom took over. I stopped for a few seconds and took deep breaths, in and out. After a few minutes, I returned to myself and was able to get on with my day. In our lives, we must take time to stop and breathe.

When was the last time, you stopped to knowingly breathe, so you could relax and gather yourself for the journey ahead?

_____

_____

_____

_____

_____

_____

_____

Freedom is activated by your thoughts, is released
throughout your body, and radiates from your spirit.

_____

_____

_____

_____

_____

_____

_____

_____

_____

_____

_____

_____

_____

_____

_____

_____

Your Journey to Wholeness Has Begun

Freedom is activated by your thoughts, is released
throughout your body, and radiates from your spirit.

_____

_____

_____

_____

_____

_____

_____

_____

_____

_____

_____

_____

_____

_____

_____

Your Journey to Wholeness Has Begun

Grandma-ism

What Are Your Intentions?

When I was a teenager, a young man came to visit me and my grandmother asked "What are your intentions toward my granddaughter?" I was a little embarrassed, and my siblings and I glanced at each other, thinking, *Here we go again.* We called it 'Grandma giving our guests the fifth degree.' What we didn't know then was that Grandma was focusing on the intentions (of the heart). She asked a key question, likely one the guests weren't able to answer. Today, I find myself asking the same question of myself in various circumstances. What are my intentions?

I challenge you to ask yourself: What are your intentions for your life, your vocation, your relationships, and your future? By answering this, you will begin to create wholeness.

_____

_____

_____

_____

_____

Freedom is activated by your thoughts, is released
throughout your body, and radiates from your spirit.

_____

_____

_____

_____

_____

_____

_____

_____

_____

_____

_____

_____

_____

_____

_____

_____

Your Journey to Wholeness Has Begun

Freedom is activated by your thoughts, is released
throughout your body, and radiates from your spirit.

_____

_____

_____

_____

_____

_____

_____

_____

_____

_____

_____

_____

_____

_____

_____

Your Journey to Wholeness Has Begun

You Heard Me, but Are You Listening?

We all hear many things each day, from various sources. How much of what we hear do we listen to? Hearing automatically happens unless there is an impairment. Listening, however, requires that what is heard is processed (concentrated on) and meaning is derived from it.

Are you a solid listener or do you simply hear? Listening involves meaning-making. Share something important you heard but did not listen to, and share the outcome. What was your lesson?

_____

_____

_____

_____

_____

_____

_____

_____

_____

_____

Freedom is activated by your thoughts, is released
throughout your body, and radiates from your spirit.

_____

_____

_____

_____

_____

_____

_____

_____

_____

_____

_____

_____

_____

_____

_____

Your Journey to Wholeness Has Begun

Freedom is activated by your thoughts, is released throughout your body, and radiates from your spirit.

_____

_____

_____

_____

_____

_____

_____

_____

_____

_____

_____

_____

_____

_____

Your Journey to Wholeness Has Begun

The Old Has Passed, the New Is Come

Past, present, and future. As we start a new year
or season in your life, many are considering
resolutions. I used to be one of those people. I no
longer make resolutions. I do, however, create
specific goals for myself each year. My goals are
specific and time-bound. I also create strategies
for how I will accomplish my goals. It is true that
the old has passed and the new has come…the
present. In this present moment, LIVE, LOVE, and
MULTIPLY.

Have you laid to rest the old? Are you taking
advantage of the present moments and
opportunities?

_____

_____

_____

_____

_____

_____

_____

_____

Freedom is activated by your thoughts, is released
throughout your body, and radiates from your spirit.

_____

_____

_____

_____

_____

_____

_____

_____

_____

_____

_____

_____

_____

_____

_____

Your Journey to Wholeness Has Begun

Freedom is activated by your thoughts, is released throughout your body, and radiates from your spirit.

_____

_____

_____

_____

_____

_____

_____

_____

_____

_____

_____

_____

_____

_____

_____

_____

Your Journey to Wholeness Has Begun

Love Matters More

When it's all said and done, what really matters? I'm not sure I'll remember all the names of people I have met, or all the places I've travelled to, or even all the foods I've enjoyed during my lifetime. I will remember love because it matters more. It's the most important thing!

Who have you loved? Forgive today. Don't wait until someday; tell it today. "Love covers a multitude of sins" (The Holy Bible). Speak in love to someone you know today or to someone who needs to hear it.

How will you do it and who will you share your 'love' with?

_____

_____

_____

_____

_____

_____

_____

Freedom is activated by your thoughts, is released
throughout your body, and radiates from your spirit.

_____

_____

_____

_____

_____

_____

_____

_____

_____

_____

_____

_____

_____

_____

Your Journey to Wholeness Has Begun

Freedom is activated by your thoughts, is released throughout your body, and radiates from your spirit.

_____

_____

_____

_____

_____

_____

_____

_____

_____

_____

_____

_____

_____

_____

_____

Your Journey to Wholeness Has Begun

Grandma-ism

Lesser Visits Make the Best of Friends

Yes, this is another grandma-ism. My grandmother did not believe that friends needed to be in and out of each other's homes quite so frequently. She believed in fewer phone calls and visits between friends. She never said why, but I didn't agree with her at the time. Now that I am older, I understand. Just look at Reality TV shows and see that friendships are often based on the appearance of things, not necessarily on truth and character of all involved. As I become older and wiser, I realize I have Jesus, a handful of faithful friends (on earth), and my sisters. We do not chat every day, but we trust and support each other. These are my 'ride or die' folks.

Who are your friends, the ones you can count on and will trust to enrich your character or make you a better person?

_____

_____

_____

_____

Freedom is activated by your thoughts, is released
throughout your body, and radiates from your spirit.

_____

_____

_____

_____

_____

_____

_____

_____

_____

_____

_____

_____

_____

_____

Your Journey to Wholeness Has Begun

Freedom is activated by your thoughts, is released
throughout your body, and radiates from your spirit.

_____

_____

_____

_____

_____

_____

_____

_____

_____

_____

_____

_____

_____

_____

_____

Your Journey to Wholeness Has Begun

Grandma-ism

Feed her with a Long-handled Spoon

Don't let that one get too close to you. Keep her at a distance, hence the long-handled spoon. This would have likely applied to someone who was a little sneaky, overly-friendly, and always trying to know all your business. Be careful who you allow in your inner circle of friends. Not everyone who appears to be for you IS actually in your corner. If friendship is based on what someone can do for you or only on what you can do for them, question the friendship.

Are there some in your inner circle who need to exit? Who are your closest, trust-worthy friends, and how do you all help each other grow and make each other better?

_____

_____

_____

_____

_____

_____

Freedom is activated by your thoughts, is released
throughout your body, and radiates from your spirit.

_____

_____

_____

_____

_____

_____

_____

_____

_____

_____

_____

_____

_____

_____

_____

Your Journey to Wholeness Has Begun

Freedom is activated by your thoughts, is released throughout your body, and radiates from your spirit.

_____

_____

_____

_____

_____

_____

_____

_____

_____

_____

_____

_____

_____

_____

_____

Your Journey to Wholeness Has Begun

Stop Telling Me and Show Me

Have you ever had someone in your life who talks a really good game? They have lots of ideas and talk a lot, but there is rarely any evidence of what they say. In short, there is no fruit.

Are you someone who talks a lot, but there is no proof of all your talk? Change that today! Write down one thing you long to do and begin writing down steps you can take to bring it to fruition.

_____

_____

_____

_____

_____

_____

_____

_____

_____

_____

_____

Freedom is activated by your thoughts, is released
throughout your body, and radiates from your spirit.

_____

_____

_____

_____

_____

_____

_____

_____

_____

_____

_____

_____

_____

_____

_____

Your Journey to Wholeness Has Begun

Freedom is activated by your thoughts, is released
throughout your body, and radiates from your spirit.

_____

_____

_____

_____

_____

_____

_____

_____

_____

_____

_____

_____

_____

_____

_____

Your Journey to Wholeness Has Begun

You Don't Need to Impress Anyone

How many times have you tried to impress others with your wit, knowledge, skills, and gifts? We're human, so that's what we sometimes do.

So what was the result? Did it make you feel better? Likely it did, but only for a moment. Next time you're faced with such a situation, rest assured you don't need to impress anyone but do commit to being your best self in every situation. Set your intention and good will follow.

_____

_____

_____

_____

_____

_____

_____

_____

_____

_____

Freedom is activated by your thoughts, is released
throughout your body, and radiates from your spirit.

_____

_____

_____

_____

_____

_____

_____

_____

_____

_____

_____

_____

_____

_____

_____

Your Journey to Wholeness Has Begun

Freedom is activated by your thoughts, is released
throughout your body, and radiates from your spirit.

_____

_____

_____

_____

_____

_____

_____

_____

_____

_____

_____

_____

_____

_____

Your Journey to Wholeness Has Begun

Change Is Your Choice

I know someone who constantly complains. It seems as if no matter what's happening, she is the victim. I do not get a chance to speak that often, so I settle in to listen, not expecting to get a word in. Finally, I suggested that if she doesn't like the way she's being treated, that she make a choice to choose the change she wants and to set boundaries.

Are there areas in your life where you need to set boundaries, so you can experience joy?

_____

_____

_____

_____

_____

_____

_____

_____

_____

_____

Freedom is activated by your thoughts, is released
throughout your body, and radiates from your spirit.

Your Journey to Wholeness Has Begun

Freedom is activated by your thoughts, is released
throughout your body, and radiates from your spirit.

_____

_____

_____

_____

_____

_____

_____

_____

_____

_____

_____

_____

_____

_____

_____

Your Journey to Wholeness Has Begun

Encourage Yourself

Have you ever needed someone to encourage you concerning a difficult situation? What if your encourager wasn't around? Practice taking some steps to encourage yourself. Say something great to yourself, even if you're looking in the mirror. Write down three great things you would say to lift your spirits and get yourself back on the path to joy!

_____

_____

_____

_____

_____

_____

_____

_____

_____

_____

Freedom is activated by your thoughts, is released
throughout your body, and radiates from your spirit.

_____

_____

_____

_____

_____

_____

_____

_____

_____

_____

_____

_____

_____

_____

_____

Your Journey to Wholeness Has Begun

Freedom is activated by your thoughts, is released throughout your body, and radiates from your spirit.

_____

_____

_____

_____

_____

_____

_____

_____

_____

_____

_____

_____

_____

_____

_____

_____

Your Journey to Wholeness Has Begun

This is What I Do, Not Who I Am

Sometimes our roles and responsibilities take on a larger part of who we are. We somehow become the title, the office, or the responsibility. It's good advice to know who you are, deep down inside, and not confuse what you do, with who you are.

When have you confused the two, and how do you stay true to who you are?

_____

_____

_____

_____

_____

_____

_____

_____

_____

_____

_____

Freedom is activated by your thoughts, is released throughout your body, and radiates from your spirit.

_____

_____

_____

_____

_____

_____

_____

_____

_____

_____

_____

_____

_____

_____

_____

Your Journey to Wholeness Has Begun

Freedom is activated by your thoughts, is released
throughout your body, and radiates from your spirit.

_____

_____

_____

_____

_____

_____

_____

_____

_____

_____

_____

_____

_____

_____

_____

Your Journey to Wholeness Has Begun

Positively Contagious

I met someone the other day who had such a positive outlook on life. Interestingly enough, she was battling a chronic illness but was not focused on the disease. She only focused on what was good and her ability to smile, laugh, and spread some cheer.

What area of your life could use some joy, despite the temporary struggles you're facing? How will you choose to do to express peace and happiness?

_____

_____

_____

_____

_____

_____

_____

_____

_____

_____

Freedom is activated by your thoughts, is released
throughout your body, and radiates from your spirit.

_____

_____

_____

_____

_____

_____

_____

_____

_____

_____

_____

_____

_____

_____

Your Journey to Wholeness Has Begun

Freedom is activated by your thoughts, is released
throughout your body, and radiates from your spirit.

_____

_____

_____

_____

_____

_____

_____

_____

_____

_____

_____

_____

_____

_____

_____

Your Journey to Wholeness Has Begun

Hang In There, Girlie

This is a quip by my mother-in-law, Beatrice. Did I mention that she is almost 92 years old? She has been a treasure to me. She had a special relationship with my Grandma Janie, so I value her and her encouraging words. No matter the situation, hang in there.

Are there times when you felt like you couldn't survive? How did you manage it? Do all you can, and then turn it over to the Lord.

_____

_____

_____

_____

_____

_____

_____

_____

_____

Freedom is activated by your thoughts, is released
throughout your body, and radiates from your spirit.

_____

_____

_____

_____

_____

_____

_____

_____

_____

_____

_____

_____

_____

_____

_____

Your Journey to Wholeness Has Begun

Freedom is activated by your thoughts, is released
throughout your body, and radiates from your spirit.

_____

_____

_____

_____

_____

_____

_____

_____

_____

_____

_____

_____

_____

_____

_____

Your Journey to Wholeness Has Begun

Doing Too Much

I was facing a situation where I felt completely overwhelmed. My 'To do' List was longer than the amount of time I needed to complete everything. I knew it from the start but continued to add to my list. At one point, I stopped and said, "I'm doing too much!" I immediately began to create the 'need to do' versus the 'nice to do.' This took off some of the pressure.

When have you tried to do too much and realized you really didn't need to?

_____

_____

_____

_____

_____

_____

_____

_____

_____

_____

Freedom is activated by your thoughts, is released
throughout your body, and radiates from your spirit.

_____

_____

_____

_____

_____

_____

_____

_____

_____

_____

_____

_____

_____

_____

Your Journey to Wholeness Has Begun

Freedom is activated by your thoughts, is released throughout your body, and radiates from your spirit.

_____

_____

_____

_____

_____

_____

_____

_____

_____

_____

_____

_____

_____

_____

_____

_____

Your Journey to Wholeness Has Begun

Grandma-ism

Folks will talk about you, as sure as you're born.

This quip is by Mrs. Irene and it is what it says it is. No matter who you are, if you're alive, folks will find something to say about you, good or bad. The moral here is don't sweat it. Let them talk. You know the truth about you and of course, God knows, so keep it moving.

What have you heard said about you?

_____

_____

_____

_____

_____

_____

_____

_____

_____

Freedom is activated by your thoughts, is released
throughout your body, and radiates from your spirit.

_____

_____

_____

_____

_____

_____

_____

_____

_____

_____

_____

_____

_____

_____

_____

Your Journey to Wholeness Has Begun

Freedom is activated by your thoughts, is released
throughout your body, and radiates from your spirit.

_____

_____

_____

_____

_____

_____

_____

_____

_____

_____

_____

_____

_____

_____

_____

Your Journey to Wholeness Has Begun

No Advice, but If I Were You, I Would...

My mom had a way of listening to me and at the end of my sharing, she would never give advice. When I asked her what she thought, she would say, "If I were you, I would...but you do what you think is best." That was probably the best advice she wouldn't give me because it made me think deeply about how she might handle it. Of course, I trusted her to handle it appropriately.

When have you listened to wise counsel and did a 'rethink' to resolve an issue or approach a decision?

_____

_____

_____

_____

_____

_____

_____

_____

Freedom is activated by your thoughts, is released
throughout your body, and radiates from your spirit.

_____

_____

_____

_____

_____

_____

_____

_____

_____

_____

_____

_____

_____

_____

_____

Your Journey to Wholeness Has Begun

Freedom is activated by your thoughts, is released throughout your body, and radiates from your spirit.

_____

_____

_____

_____

_____

_____

_____

_____

_____

_____

_____

_____

_____

_____

_____

Your Journey to Wholeness Has Begun

The Lord is in Control

My mother-in-law, Beatrice, shares this quip often. It's a reminder that God has each of us in the palm of His hands. We often think that we have control, but I heard someone say once that control is an illusion. That being the case, we pray, we praise, and we give our problems, issues, and concerns over to the Lord.

What do you need to surrender to the Lord?

_____

_____

_____

_____

_____

_____

_____

_____

_____

_____

Freedom is activated by your thoughts, is released throughout your body, and radiates from your spirit.

_____

_____

_____

_____

_____

_____

_____

_____

_____

_____

_____

_____

_____

_____

Your Journey to Wholeness Has Begun

Freedom is activated by your thoughts, is released
throughout your body, and radiates from your spirit.

_____

_____

_____

_____

_____

_____

_____

_____

_____

_____

_____

_____

_____

_____

_____

Your Journey to Wholeness Has Begun

Enough

There are moments, when I've doubted myself. There are times, when I allowed fear to stop me from doing things that I wanted to do. Why? I questioned whether I was enough. Guess what? I AM ENOUGH and SO ARE YOU! We are fully capable to getting 'it' done, so why fret? Stand in the face of fear and move past it, as though it was a tap on the shoulder.

What has you frozen in fear today? Tell it that you are enough NOW!

_____

_____

_____

_____

_____

_____

_____

_____

_____

Freedom is activated by your thoughts, is released
throughout your body, and radiates from your spirit.

_____

_____

_____

_____

_____

_____

_____

_____

_____

_____

_____

_____

_____

_____

Your Journey to Wholeness Has Begun

Freedom is activated by your thoughts, is released
throughout your body, and radiates from your spirit.

_____

_____

_____

_____

_____

_____

_____

_____

_____

_____

_____

_____

_____

_____

Your Journey to Wholeness Has Begun

Grandma-ism

God Don't Like Ugly and He Ain't Too Fond of Pretty.

I suppose you're curious about this quip from my Grandma Annie, huh? Well, it simply means that God does not look favorably upon the mistreatment or wrong-doing against others, no matter who you are. If you're wrong, admit it. Ask forgiveness or make amends.

When have you acted ugly and needed to make amends? If you haven't already, handle that TODAY!

_____

_____

_____

_____

_____

_____

_____

Freedom is activated by your thoughts, is released
throughout your body, and radiates from your spirit.

_____

_____

_____

_____

_____

_____

_____

_____

_____

_____

_____

_____

_____

_____

_____

Your Journey to Wholeness Has Begun

Freedom is activated by your thoughts, is released
throughout your body, and radiates from your spirit.

_____

_____

_____

_____

_____

_____

_____

_____

_____

_____

_____

_____

_____

_____

_____

Your Journey to Wholeness Has Begun

Possibilities

I have always believed that possibilities exist to make life better for me, for my family, and for others. No matter what's happening around me, I always see light at the end of it and can think of ways to succeed, even if I have to think critically of ways to work around that which causes a problem.

What problem have you been able to solve because you could imagine possibilities?

_____

_____

_____

_____

_____

_____

_____

_____

_____

_____

Freedom is activated by your thoughts, is released throughout your body, and radiates from your spirit.

_____

_____

_____

_____

_____

_____

_____

_____

_____

_____

_____

_____

_____

_____

_____

Your Journey to Wholeness Has Begun

Freedom is activated by your thoughts, is released
throughout your body, and radiates from your spirit.

_____

_____

_____

_____

_____

_____

_____

_____

_____

_____

_____

_____

_____

_____

_____

Your Journey to Wholeness Has Begun

Self-Examination

Have you ever looked through a microscope and saw things you never would have seen at first glance or without the aid of a magnifier? The same is true for your life. Each of us must examine our motives, actions, and beliefs daily. In doing that, we are able to achieve greatness, not only the ordinary.

Share an example of a time when you've envisioned or achieved more, simply because of self-examination.

_____

_____

_____

_____

_____

_____

_____

_____

_____

_____

Freedom is activated by your thoughts, is released
throughout your body, and radiates from your spirit.

_____

_____

_____

_____

_____

_____

_____

_____

_____

_____

_____

_____

_____

_____

Your Journey to Wholeness Has Begun

Freedom is activated by your thoughts, is released throughout your body, and radiates from your spirit.

_____

_____

_____

_____

_____

_____

_____

_____

_____

_____

_____

_____

_____

_____

_____

Your Journey to Wholeness Has Begun

Grandma-ism

You're a Ram in the Bush

I am not sure if you know the Bible story of how God provided a sacrifice for Abraham, but God provided the sacrifice only at the last minute. This would be considered a moment of rescue. Grandma Janie coined this one.

Have you ever felt that you needed someone to rescue you from something you were not capable of rescuing yourself from? How did you handle it and what was the outcome?

_____

_____

_____

_____

_____

_____

_____

_____

Freedom is activated by your thoughts, is released
throughout your body, and radiates from your spirit.

_____

_____

_____

_____

_____

_____

_____

_____

_____

_____

_____

_____

_____

_____

_____

Your Journey to Wholeness Has Begun

Freedom is activated by your thoughts, is released throughout your body, and radiates from your spirit.

_____

_____

_____

_____

_____

_____

_____

_____

_____

_____

_____

_____

_____

_____

_____

Your Journey to Wholeness Has Begun

Disappointment or Opportunity?

It's all in how you look at it. Perspective can make or break you or some challenging situation you are facing. Change your perspective. See the challenge from a place of abundance, not from a place of lack.

Share a challenge you have faced and how you overcame it.

_____

_____

_____

_____

_____

_____

_____

_____

_____

_____

_____

Freedom is activated by your thoughts, is released
throughout your body, and radiates from your spirit.

_____

_____

_____

_____

_____

_____

_____

_____

_____

_____

_____

_____

_____

_____

Your Journey to Wholeness Has Begun

Freedom is activated by your thoughts, is released
throughout your body, and radiates from your spirit.

_____

_____

_____

_____

_____

_____

_____

_____

_____

_____

_____

_____

_____

_____

_____

Your Journey to Wholeness Has Begun

Grandma-ism

You Don't Miss Your Water Until Your Well Runs Dry

Ever forgot about how good things are until they no longer exist? This anecdote reminds us to appreciate and be grateful for what we have. Sometimes we forget.

What have you forgotten about that you want or need to be more thankful for?

_____

_____

_____

_____

_____

_____

_____

_____

_____

_____

Freedom is activated by your thoughts, is released
throughout your body, and radiates from your spirit.

_____

_____

_____

_____

_____

_____

_____

_____

_____

_____

_____

_____

_____

_____

_____

_____

Your Journey to Wholeness Has Begun

Freedom is activated by your thoughts, is released
throughout your body, and radiates from your spirit.

_____

_____

_____

_____

_____

_____

_____

_____

_____

_____

_____

_____

_____

_____

_____

A Season of Peace

Seasons change, perspectives change, and sometimes people change. Of course, change is a choice. A choice that is lived out through actions. A season of peace exists when you are no longer content with the ordinary, but choose peace.

Have you ever experienced a peace that goes beyond all expectation? I have and it is wonderful! How can you achieve it? Find a quiet place and spend time thinking of all the simple things you can be grateful for.

_____

_____

_____

_____

_____

_____

_____

_____

_____

Freedom is activated by your thoughts, is released
throughout your body, and radiates from your spirit.

_____

_____

_____

_____

_____

_____

_____

_____

_____

_____

_____

_____

_____

_____

_____

_____

Your Journey to Wholeness Has Begun

Freedom is activated by your thoughts, is released
throughout your body, and radiates from your spirit.

Your Journey to Wholeness Has Begun

Grandma-ism

You're Going from Pillar to Post

Ever got so busy that you feel like the little hamster on the wheel? I think we all have experienced this from time to time. My Grandma Janie would have called that 'going from pillar to post' and getting nowhere fast. Take a pause.

What do you need to slow down?

_____

_____

_____

_____

_____

_____

_____

_____

_____

_____

Freedom is activated by your thoughts, is released throughout your body, and radiates from your spirit.

_____

_____

_____

_____

_____

_____

_____

_____

_____

_____

_____

_____

_____

_____

_____

Your Journey to Wholeness Has Begun

Freedom is activated by your thoughts, is released
throughout your body, and radiates from your spirit.

_____

_____

_____

_____

_____

_____

_____

_____

_____

_____

_____

_____

_____

_____

_____

Your Journey to Wholeness Has Begun

Grandma-ism

Let the Life I live Speak for Me

I attended a funeral with my grandmother once. My grandmother Janie was a woman full of wisdom. She served diligently at church but rarely wanted to speak to an audience. She was asked to say a few words about Miss Emma, a neighbor who had passed away. She got up and shared a couple of stories about the friendship that existed between her and Miss Emma. Once she was done, she said, "May the life Miss Emma lived speak for her."

What will the life you are living, say about you? If you aren't satisfied with your answer, write what you will change, so your life speaks what you would want to hear.

_____

_____

_____

_____

_____

_____

Freedom is activated by your thoughts, is released
throughout your body, and radiates from your spirit.

_____

_____

_____

_____

_____

_____

_____

_____

_____

_____

_____

_____

_____

_____

Your Journey to Wholeness Has Begun

Freedom is activated by your thoughts, is released throughout your body, and radiates from your spirit.

_____

_____

_____

_____

_____

_____

_____

_____

_____

_____

_____

_____

_____

_____

Your Journey to Wholeness Has Begun

Love Notes & Acknowledgements

All that I am, as a woman who is on this
journey to becoming WHOLE, is due to God
the Father, Son, and Holy Spirit. A special
thanks to the following women for their
precious contributions:

My Mom, Hattie

****

My Maternal Grandma, Janie

****

My Paternal Grandma, Annie

****

My Mother-in-Law, Beatrice

****

My Best Friend's Mom, Mrs. Irene

****

These ladies will forever be in my heart and
their words of knowledge are a part of legacy
for those who are coming after us. I thank

God for placing them in my life and for the impartation of wisdom.

Thanks to God for His vision, creativity, ideas, promptings, and full manifestation of purpose in my life. With God, all things are possible!

Who are you thankful for today? Who has had an impact on the WHOLE person you are becoming?

_____

_____

_____

_____

_____

_____

_____

_____

_____

_____

_____

_____

_____

_____

Who are you thankful for today? Who has had an
impact on the WHOLE person you are
becoming?

_____

_____

_____

_____

_____

_____

_____

_____

_____

_____

_____

_____

_____

_____

Dr. Sanders–Funnye may be reached for Training & Development, Workshops, Conferences, and Consultation at:

Drfunnye1@gmail.com

Made in the USA
Middletown, DE
13 April 2022

64219101R00086